# HOW TO BE
## A
# WITCH

To the East Camp Kids (and their minders)
for always seeking to be the best version of themselves!
–GSB
For Aunt Carole who has always bewitched me
with her curiosity and bravery.
–SG
Para David y Maria mis brujas favoritas.
–CS

We are so grateful to witches past, present, and future
and for the counsel of Jeni Wrightson, Hudson Valley Warrior Witch.

RISE x Penguin Workshop
An imprint of Penguin Random House LLC
1745 Broadway, New York, New York 10019

First published in the United States of America by Rise × Penguin Workshop, an imprint of
Penguin Random House LLC, 2024

Text copyright © 2024 by Gabrielle Balkan and Shana Gozansky
Illustrations copyright © 2024 by Carmen Saldaña

Visit us online at penguinrandomhouse.com.

Library of Congress Cataloging-in-Publication Data is available.

Manufactured in China

ISBN 9780593751190          10 9 8 7 6 5 4 3 2 1 HH

The text is set in Big Mamma.
The art was created by mixing digital and traditional paint.

Edited by Cecily Kaiser
Designed by Rae Peckman

# HOW TO BE
## — A —
# WITCH

words by
**Gabrielle Balkan
& Shana Gozansky**

art by
**Carmen Saldaña**

RISE

NEW YORK

Did you know that witches are real?
It's true! Only *pretend* witches have green skin,
pointy hats, and fly on broomsticks.

What do real witches look like?
What do they wear? What do they do?
Let's find out!

# Which one is a real witch?

Is she a witch?

Are they a witch?

What about these two?

Guess what? They are all witches!
Witches are people who learn and practice magic,
and use their magic to help and to heal.

Witches can be young, old, big, or small.
They can have dark skin or light skin.
Lots of hair or none at all.

It doesn't matter what you look like.
Anyone can be a witch—even you!

What makes a witch a witch?
How do you know if you want to be one?

Well, do you love nature?
Do you like helping others?
Do you believe magic is real?
Do you like learning new things?

If you answered yes, then you have
what it takes to become a witch.

Witches practice magic through spells
and potions, as a way to help others.
There are many different types of witches!
Here are a few:

**Crystal Witch**

**Kitchen Witch**

**Green Witch**

**Cosmic Witch**

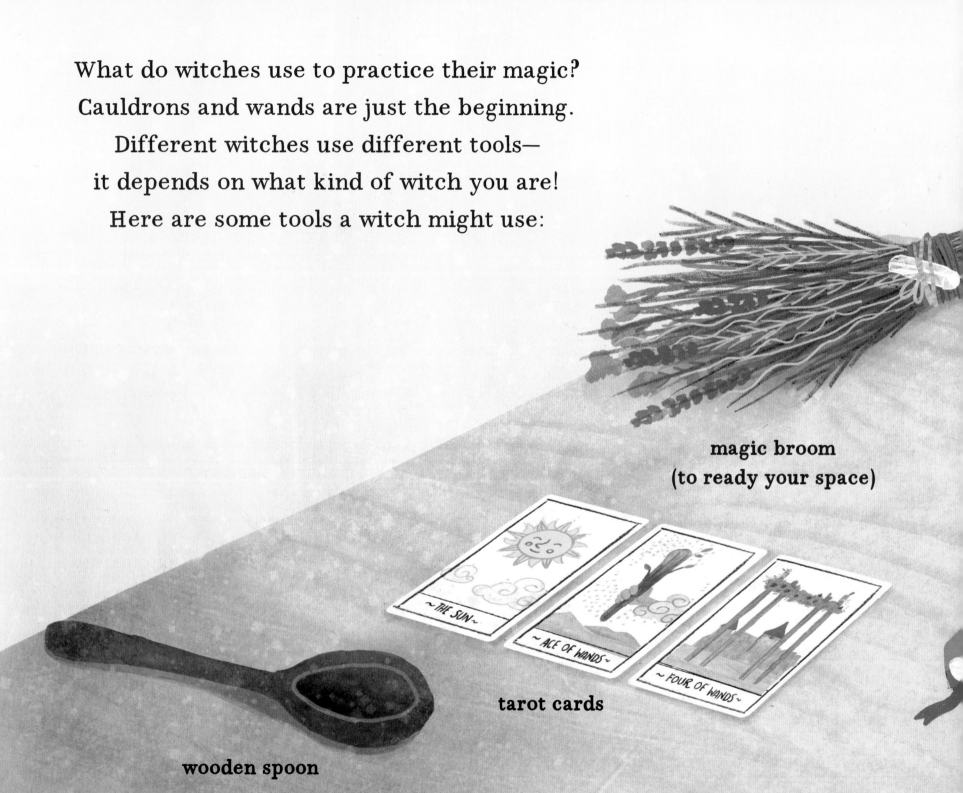

What do witches use to practice their magic?
Cauldrons and wands are just the beginning.
Different witches use different tools—
it depends on what kind of witch you are!
Here are some tools a witch might use:

magic broom
(to ready your space)

tarot cards

~THE SUN~

~ACE OF WANDS~

~FOUR OF WANDS~

wooden spoon

cleaning-up broom
(for when you're all done)

candles

crystals

spell book

notebook and pen

Casting a spell is one way that witches
make magic. A spell can be a poem,
a song, a chant, or even a whisper!

Witches cast spells to help someone
else, or to help themselves.
A spell is a special way for a witch
to share their love, thank someone,
or say they want to help.

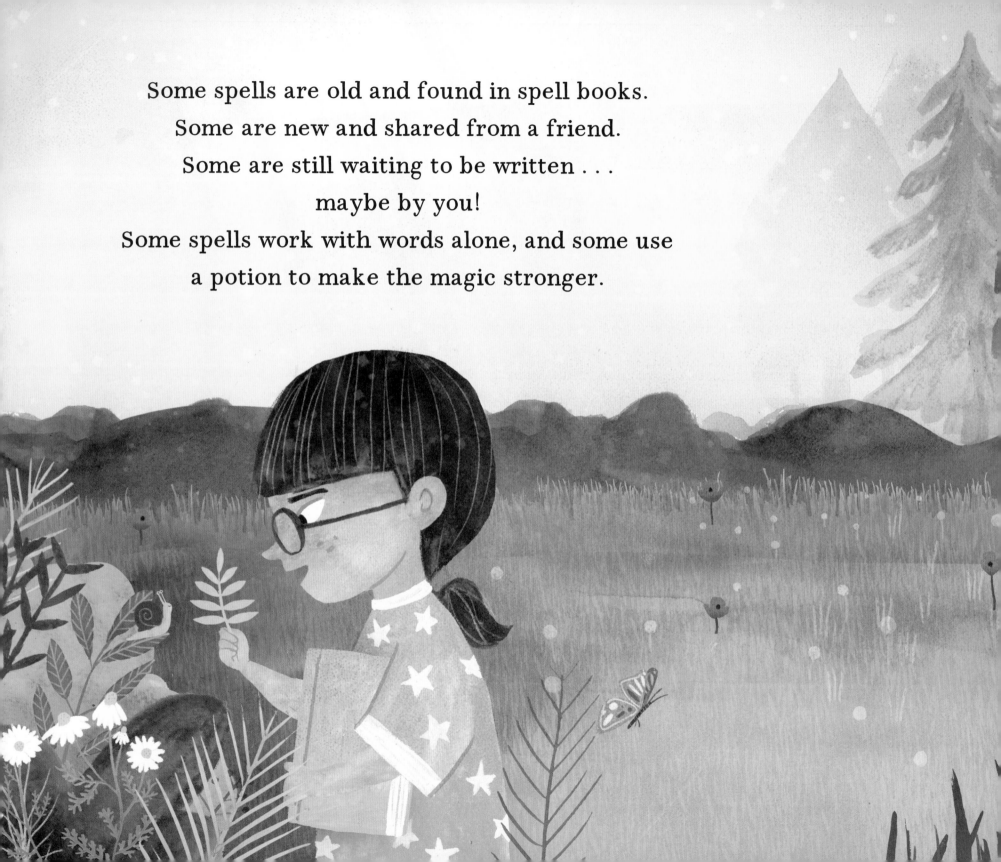

Some spells are old and found in spell books.
Some are new and shared from a friend.
Some are still waiting to be written . . .
maybe by you!
Some spells work with words alone, and some use
a potion to make the magic stronger.

Potions are a magical way to bring nature and
humans together. Potions come in many forms and have
different uses. Some can heal an upset tummy.
Others can help a worried friend. Whatever you need,
there is probably a potion for it.

Witches pick herbs, witches mix herbs, witches cook
up something special—a tea brewed in a favorite mug to
comfort, or fresh-baked bread to honor the earth; a bundle
of lavender to calm someone who's troubled, or flowers and
herbs sprinkled over a bath to delight the senses.

Pigeon's Grass

**vervain**
**helps with headaches**

Elf Leaf

**lavender**
*relieves stress*

Witches find their magic recipes in books
of potions, or create their own recipes to
experiment with new kinds of magic.

*Eye of Newt*

**wild mustard seed**
helps with healing

*Dew of the Sea*

**rosemary**
warms the body

Witches use ingredients from their kitchens,
or go out into nature to see what they can find.
Some herbs have nicknames that describe what
they look like or where they are found.

Do witches work alone? Sometimes.
Other times, they work with magical friends.

A magical friend can be another witch. A group
of witches that work together is called a coven.

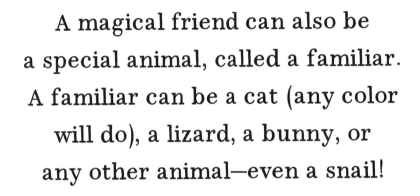

A magical friend can also be
a special animal, called a familiar.
A familiar can be a cat (any color
will do), a lizard, a bunny, or
any other animal—even a snail!

Whatever the animal, they
are more than your pet.
They are your partner in magic.

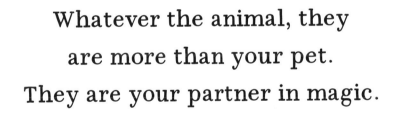

# What does a witch wear?

Whatever they want!

They can stomp around in big boots, dance
in bare feet, wear flower crowns or shell necklaces,
put on fancy suits or a cozy cloak.

Witches dress to feel powerful, strong, and brave.

Where do witches live?
Anywhere, everywhere, all around the world!
Some live near snow-capped mountains or rocky deserts.
Others live in quiet woods or noisy cities.

Apartments, cabins, trailers,
or houses—witches make magic
wherever they call home.

Do witches practice magic all day?

Sometimes! But not always.

Witches have things to do
just like everyone else!

And then, when that's done . . .

A witch might visit the ocean,
tend to a garden, walk through a forest,
or track the phases of the moon.

All witches spend time with nature.
Nature strengthens the magic inside a witch.

There's magic inside you, too.
You are brave and bold, creative and smart, caring
and powerful, just as all witches are. So . . .

Step out into nature, gather your tools, stir up your potions, create your spells, focus your mind, feel your power, and share your magic with the world!

# Share Your Magic with the World

Would you like to try some magic?
We wrote a gratitude spell and potion just for you. Use them as they are,
or let them inspire you to create a spell and potion of your very own.

—— GRATITUDE SPELL ——

Say this out loud—on your own, with a friend, or repeating after a grown-up.

I thank the sun for its warming energy,

the moon for its cool cast of light.

I thank my friends for their laughter and play,

my family for our cozy, loving life.

I thank myself for being curious and brave.

To the stars, the seas, creatures big and small,

thank you, thank you, thank you, thank you to all.

Now you can make the spell your own! Complete the following spell with details that are important to you. Write your spell in your spell book.

I thank the _____ for its _____ ,
_____something in nature that helps you_____ _____describe part of that thing_____

the _____ for its _____ .
_____something in nature that you enjoy_____ _____describe part of that thing_____

I thank my friends for _____
_____something helpful that a friend does_____

and _____ ,
_____something you enjoy about a friend_____

my family for _____
_____something about your family that helps you_____

and _____ .
_____something about your family that you enjoy_____

I thank myself for being _____
_____something about yourself that makes you proud_____

and _____ .
_____something about yourself that is unique_____

To the _____ , the _____ ,
_____something in nature that helps you_____ _____something in nature that you enjoy_____

_____ ,
_____something in nature that inspires you_____

thank you, thank you, thank you, thank you to all.

## — FULL MOON GRATITUDE POTION —

## First, gather what you need:

### A glass jar with a lid

An empty spice or jelly jar works well!
This is your cauldron. You can decorate your jar
with stickers, gems, and things you have found
in nature, like a dried flower or feather.

### Some cooking oil

Like olive, avocado, canola—whatever food-safe
oil you have in your kitchen will do!

### Some herbs or spices, fresh or dried

Such as sage, lavender, cinnamon, cloves—
choose ones that smell good to you.

### A few things from nature

Such as flower petals, an interesting leaf, a
curious shell, a special rock. Never use a living
insect or animal. Check with a grown-up to
make sure you are not collecting anything that
might irritate your skin.

Then, assemble your potion and cast your spell:

1. Mix everything together in the jar while thinking about what you are grateful for. When you finish, make sure the lid is on tight!

2. Place your potion on a windowsill.
   Let it bathe overnight in the light of the full moon.

3. When the sun rises, your gratitude potion is ready.

4. Place a drop of your potion on your wrist or behind your ear.
   (Wipe it off with a wet washcloth if you don't like the way it feels.)

5. To make the magic stronger, recite your gratitude spell.

---

Always check with a grown-up before you start making any potions
or lighting any candles. And note: This potion is NOT edible!

# More Things to Know About Witches

### Do real witches have green skin?

"Nope, not unless they are wearing face paint. The idea of witches having green skin came from the 1939 movie *The Wizard of Oz*. A pretend witch with green skin looked more interesting on a big movie screen, especially because most other movies back then were black and white." **—Gabrielle**

### Why do pretend witch costumes often include a pointed hat?

"We're not exactly sure. Many years ago, some women wore pointy hats so you could spot them (and buy the drinks they made!) in a crowded market. The idea of a pointed witch hat for a pretend witch costume may be based on that." **—Shana**

### Do real witches use a broomstick to fly from one place to another?

"No. Brooms cannot fly, unless they have a motor! Real witches use scooters, skateboards, roller skates, trains, buses, and the same sort of transportation that anyone else might use. The idea of flying broomsticks may have started hundreds of years ago, when some farmers thought it was good luck to dance and jump with a broom or pitchfork under the light of a full moon. This dance was supposed to look like corn growing and encourage the plant to grow tall!" **—Gabrielle**

### Do real witches really use spell books and potions?

"Everything in this book is from real witches who practice magic today, so, *yes!* Some witches use spells and potions, some use recipes and intentions. Witches also use old spells and potions to inspire new ones of their own." **—Shana**

### How does someone become a witch?

"There are many different paths to becoming a witch. A witch might come from a family with many generations of witches; another might be inspired by cultural traditions; and some might teach themselves. Practicing witchcraft can be something you have inherited or something someone else might inherit from you." **—Shana**